Edna Mae Burnam's PIANO COURSE

with

Close-Phased Grading

PHASE 1
Hand Positioning

THE WILLIS MUSIC COMPANY

© 1954, Revised © 1967 The Willis Music Company, Florence, KY, USA. All rights Reserved

ISBN: 978-0-7119-5682-0

For all works contained herein:
Unauthorized copying, arranging, adapting, recording, internet posting, public performance,
or other distribution of the music in this publication is an infringement of copyright.
Infringers are liable under the law.

Visit Hal Leonard Online at
www.halleonard.com

Contact us:
Hal Leonard
7777 West Bluemound Road
Milwaukee, WI 53213
Email: info@halleonard.com

In Europe, contact:
Hal Leonard Europe Limited
42 Wigmore Street
Marylebone, London, W1U 2RY
Email: info@halleonardeurope.com

In Australia, contact:
Hal Leonard Australia Pty. Ltd.
4 Lentara Court
Cheltenham, Victoria, 3192 Australia
Email: info@halleonard.com.au

FOREWORD

MINISTEPS TO MUSIC is a project that occupied my mind for a long time before the final draft was made ready for publication. The original germ of an idea, sparked off during teaching sessions with five- and six-year old piano pupils, was subjected to constant emendment, revision, expansion and duplicated "second thoughts". The outcome of this endeavour which is issued in six books will, it is hoped, meet with approbation from all who cherish being associated as teachers with the richly imaginative and fertile world of the young musician.

EDNA MAE BURNAM

To

Chris, Billy, Mona, Katie and Matthew

INTRODUCTION

MINISTEPS TO MUSIC is planned to teach the rudimentary stages of keyboard and theoretical understanding at a deliberately moderated pace. This tempo of progress has been formulated to counterbalance the many educational and occupational distractions which compete for attention from the child-mind. Reading notation, associating the printed note with its position on the keyboard, assessing the musical value of the note to be played and choosing the correct finger to depress the piano key, can be confusing to a young beginner unless this knowledge is allowed to seep gradually into his awareness. This multiplicity of points to be observed can take on a forbidding appearance, leading to a distaste on the part of the student for the graphic language of music.

CLOSE-PHASED GRADING was prompted by the difficulties met with by certain young pupils in mastering the basic essentials, as presented in the average course of piano study. Although many beginners at the piano are generally receptive to melodic impressions — usually nursery rhymes learned by rote — it is only after much repetitive toil at the instrument that the certain few are able to associate the words and airs with the appropriate music notation. The two-bar and four-bar sentence songs in **Phase I** of **MINISTEPS TO MUSIC** will train the eye to recognize the syllabic division of the words, and the ear to assess the rhythmic pulse and melodic pitch of the modest tunes. Given ample examples to perform within his reading and technical capacity, the young player acquires a freedom and decisiveness at the keyboard which suggest that **CLOSE-PHASED GRADING** promotes musical confidence and a natural development of pianistic skill.

When **Phase I** of **MINISTEPS TO MUSIC** is completed, the student will have learned:

1. How the fingers are numbered for piano playing.
2. How to recognize and name the following features of music notation:—
   treble clef — bass clef — brace — grand staff — bar-line — bar — double-bar fingering.
3. Naming and playing a group of notes in the five-finger position in the treble clef and four notes in the bass clef radiating from Middle C. Using this notation in some two-dozen little pieces.

4. The note-values of the crotchet, minim, dotted-minim, semibreve.
5. The "silence-value" of crotchet-, minim-, semibreve-rests.
6. Recognition of rhythm and pulse as defined by the following time signatures
7. The purpose of tied notes.

THIS IS HOW YOU NUMBER YOUR FINGERS FOR PLAYING THE PIANO

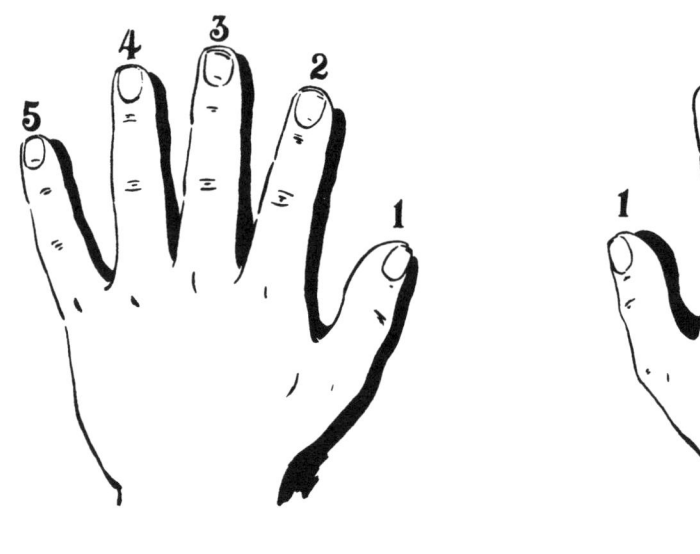
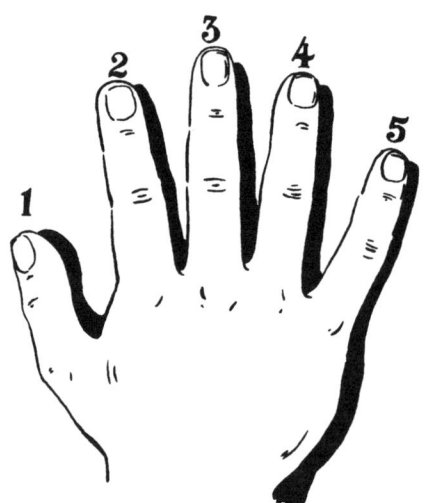

Left hand   Right hand

Note! The thumb is always marked with a figure 1

© MCMLIX, Revised © MCMLXVII by The Willis Music Co
Chappell & Co. Ltd., 50 New Bond Street, London, W.1
International Copyright Secured

HERE ARE TWO BLACK KEYS

7

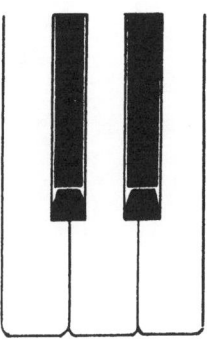

Find them on the piano

See how many groups of the two black keys you can find.

Play them one at a time and sing "One, Two".

Use any fingers you wish.

W. M. Co., 8448

MIDDLE C ON KEYBOARD

Find the WHITE note to the left of the two black keys (in the **middle** of the keyboard).

This WHITE note is named MIDDLE C.

Play it with either hand but use the FINGER MARKED 1 (thumb) as you play MIDDLE C.

Sing C as you play it.

TREBLE CLEF

This is a **treble clef** sign

Notes from MIDDLE C to the **top** of the keyboard to the **right,** are written **after** a treble clef sign.

BASS CLEF

This is a **bass clef sign**

Notes from MIDDLE C to the **bottom** of the keyboard to the **left,** are written **after** a bass clef sign.

MIDDLE C's PLAYGROUND

MIDDLE C has a wide playground.

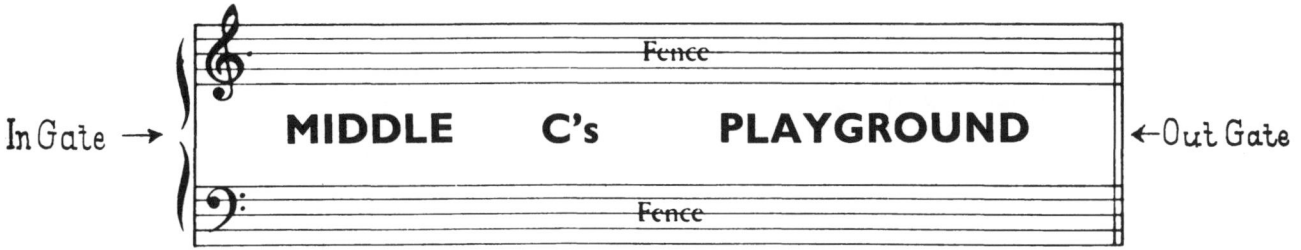

There is a fence on two sides of the playground.

There is a fancy iron gate to go **into** the playground.

There is a double-bar iron gate at the end.

MIDDLE C **never** goes out of the playground.

PICTURES OF MIDDLE C

Here are some pictures of MIDDLE C.

MIDDLE C is **always in** the playground. It may be in different parts of the playground but it cannot climb on to the fences as represented by the five-line staves.

MIDDLE C **always** has a line going through it ⟶ 𝄻   (this is called a **leger** line).

Sometimes MIDDLE C has a stem.

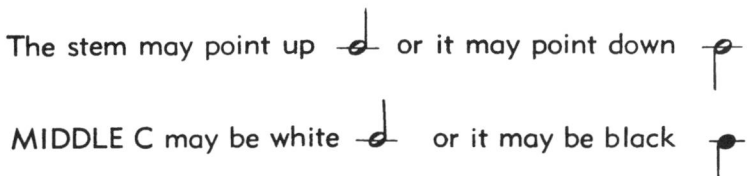

Look below and see the different pictures of MIDDLE C in the playground.

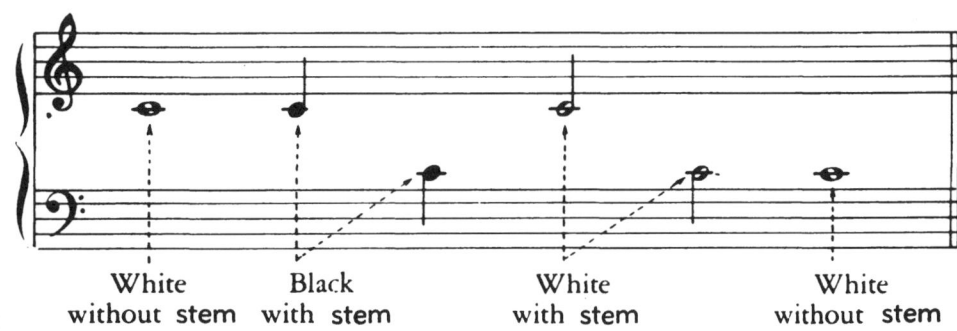

LOOK AT THE PICTURES OF MIDDLE C

Play MIDDLE C just as many times as you see it in the playground.

Use either hand you wish, but use the **finger marked 1** (thumb).

Begin at the "In Gate" and play each MIDDLE C to the "Out Gate".

Keep your eyes on the MIDDLE C's so that you will not lose your place!

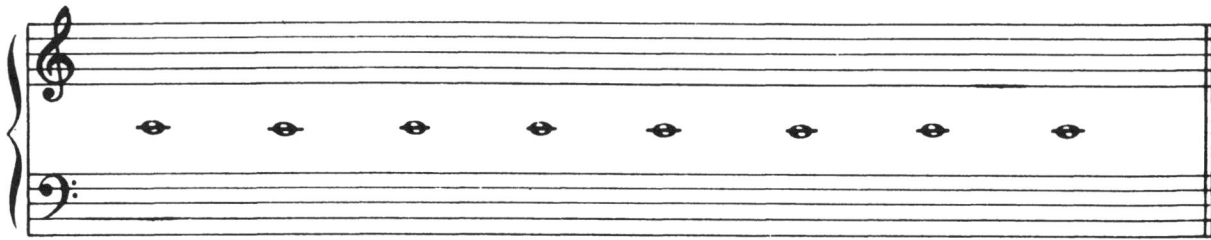

MIDDLE C WITH STEM

Here is a picture of MIDDLE C with a stem pointing **up**

Is the stem on the right or left side of MIDDLE C?

When the stem goes **up,** you must play MIDDLE C with the hand that is on the same **side** as the stem. (Your **right** hand).

Use the **finger marked 1** (thumb) of your **right** hand as you play the MIDDLE C's below.

The number 1 above MIDDLE C is a finger mark. It means to use the thumb of your right hand.

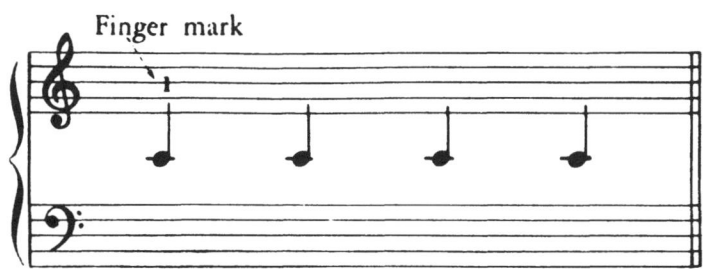

When the stem goes **down** you must play MIDDLE C with the hand that is on the same side as the stem (your **left** hand).

Use the **finger marked 1** (thumb of your **left** hand as you play the MIDDLE C's below.

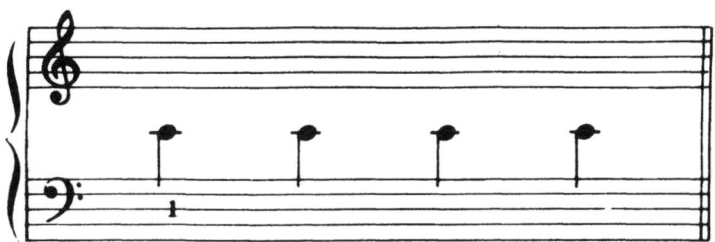

HERE ARE MORE MIDDLE C's

BE SURE YOU PLAY EACH ONE WITH THE CORRECT HAND!

BAR-LINES - DOUBLE BAR-LINES - BARS

There are lines separating MIDDLE C's playground. In music, these are called **bar-lines**.

The places **between** these bar-lines are called bars.

Notice the last heavy **double-bar**. It means we have come to the end.

How many bars are there below?

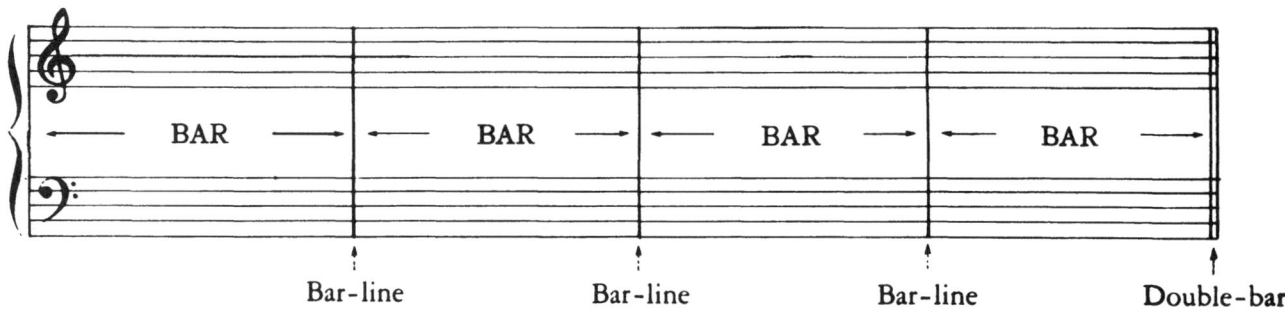

COUNT THREE KINDS OF MIDDLE C's

When MIDDLE C is **black** and has a **stem**, it sings long enough for you to count **ONE**. (This is a **crotchet**).

Play and count 1

When MIDDLE C is **white** and has a **stem**, it sings a little longer. Long enough for you to count **ONE, TWO**. (This is a **minim**).

Play and count 1, 2

When MIDDLE C is **white** and has no **stem**, it sings even **longer**. Long enough for you to count ONE, TWO, THREE, FOUR. (This is a **semibreve**).

Play and count 1, 2, 3, 4

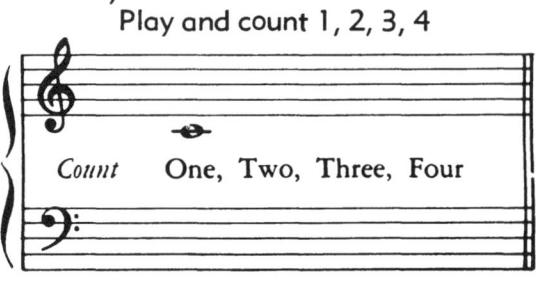

W. M. Co., 8448

$\frac{2}{4}$ TIME SIGNATURE

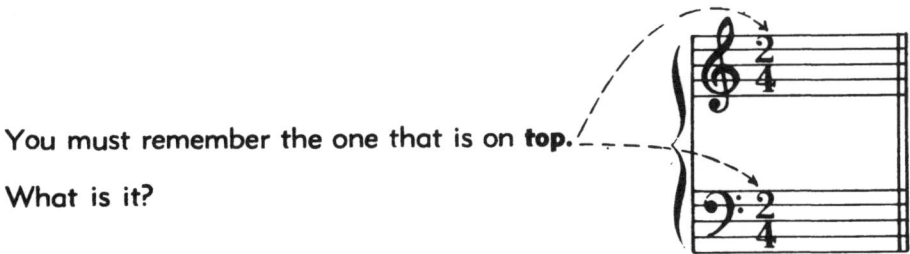

Notice the numbers on the fences (staves).

You must remember the one that is on **top**.

What is it?

It means that you must count 1, 2 in **every bar**.

These numbers are called the TIME SIGNATURE.

After every **bar-line** you must **always** begin counting ONE again.

Clap and **count** for each MIDDLE C below.
Do not stop until you reach the **double-bar** at the end.

TIP TOE

Count like this — One, Two, | One, Two, | One, Two, | One, Two

Did you remember to count, ONE, TWO in the last bar?

Now **play** and count. Use correct hands and fingers.

The name of this piece is TIP TOE, so play it evenly and without force.

When you can **play** and **count** this piece perfectly, you may sing these words:—

"Tip - toe, Tip - toe, Here I Go".

Now play TIP TOE again and your teacher will play with you.

Teacher's Part

W. M. Co., 8448

$\frac{4}{4}$ TIME SIGNATURE

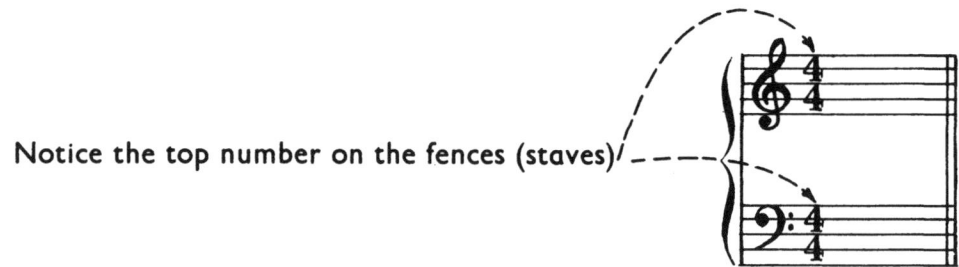

Notice the top number on the fences (staves)

This means that you must count 1, 2, 3, 4 in every bar.

Clap and count the piece named HOP and STOP.

When you can play and count it perfectly you may sing the words.

HOP and STOP

Hop and stop. Hop and stop. Hop and hop and stop.

Teacher's Part

Here is another piece for you to learn in the same way.

POP CORN

Come and have some Pop Corn, Snow-white pop-ping Pop Corn.

Teacher's Part

W. M. Co., 8448

D ON KEYBOARD

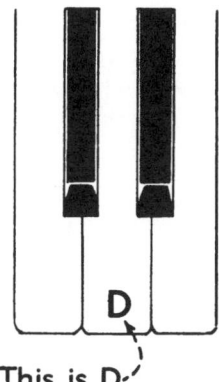

This is D

Find the next note to the **right** of Middle C (**between** the two black keys).

Play D with the **finger marked 2** of your **right** hand.

Sing "D" as you play it.

Here are some pictures of D

Remember that D is the note between the two black keys.

D does **not** have a leger line through it.

D is in Middle C's playground. It can only play in the **top** of it.

Use the second finger of your **right** hand as you play D.

Here are some pieces for you to play.

SLEEP

Sleep my ba-by Sleep.

Teacher's Part

ON THE BUS

On the bus the peo-ple tra-vel, All a-round the town.

Teacher's Part

W. M. Co., 8448

D ON KEYBOARD (Continued)

THE RAIN

Hear the gent-le rain. On the wind-ow pane.

Teacher's Part

LEAVES

Leaves are fall-ing down. All a-round the town.

Teacher's Part

B ON KEYBOARD

Find the white note to the **left** of Middle C

This is B

Play B with the **finger marked 2** of your **left** hand.

Sing "B" as you play it.

PICTURES OF B

Here are some pictures of B

B is in Middle C's playground. It can only play in the **bottom** of it.

Use the finger marked 2 of your **left** hand as you play B.

Here are some new pieces for you to play.

BOAT SONG

Rock my lit-tle boat.

Teacher's Part

THE DRUM

Rub, Dub, Dub, Rub, Dub, Dub, Hear me play my drum.

Teacher's Part

IN A HAMMOCK

Back and forth, and back and forth, and back and forth, I'm swing-ing.

Teacher's Part

W. M. Co., 8448

Here is a piece named THE WOODPECKER

Notice the third bar.

In this bar the **right** hand plays on counts 1, 2, 3, 4.

The **left** hand plays on counts 1, 2, 3, 4 **also**.

You must play with **both hands at the same time** in the third bar!

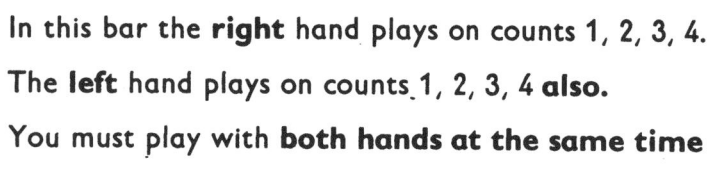

THE WOODPECKER

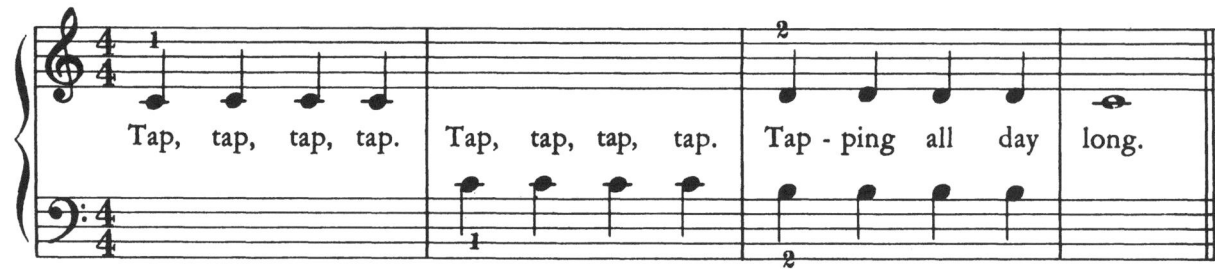

Tap, tap, tap, tap. Tap, tap, tap, tap. Tap-ping all day long.

Teacher's Part

E ON KEYBOARD

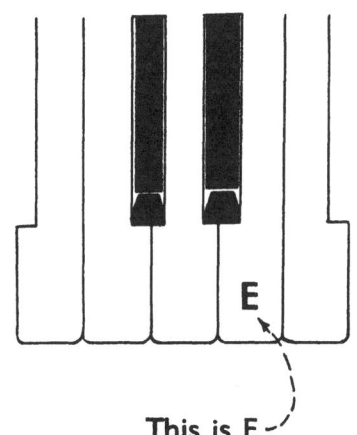

This is E

Find the white note to the **right** of D.

Play E with the **finger marked 3** of your **right** hand.

Sing E as you play it.

W. M. Co., 8448

BRACE - GRAND STAFF - STAVE

In music the treble and bass "fences" are called the grand staff. Separately they are referred to as stave or staff, being made up of lines and spaces.

This is a brace.

It holds the **treble** and **bass staves** together so that we can read notes which are playable on the entire keyboard.

The stave is made up of **lines** and **spaces**.

Here are the **lines**.

The **places between** are called **spaces**.

Usually the right hand plays notes written on the treble stave.
Such notation is generally described as being in the treble clef.

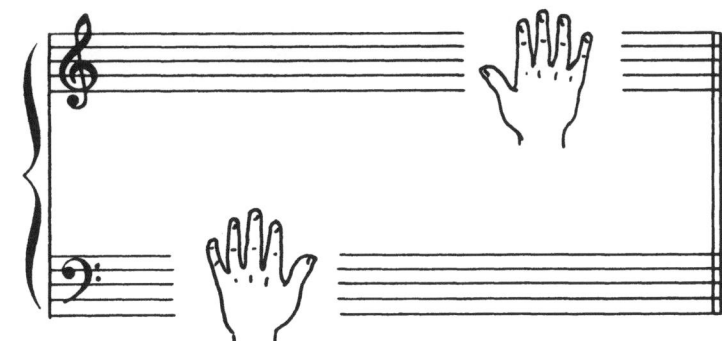

Usually the left hand plays notes written on the bass stave.
Such notation is generally described as being in the bass clef.

PICTURES OF E

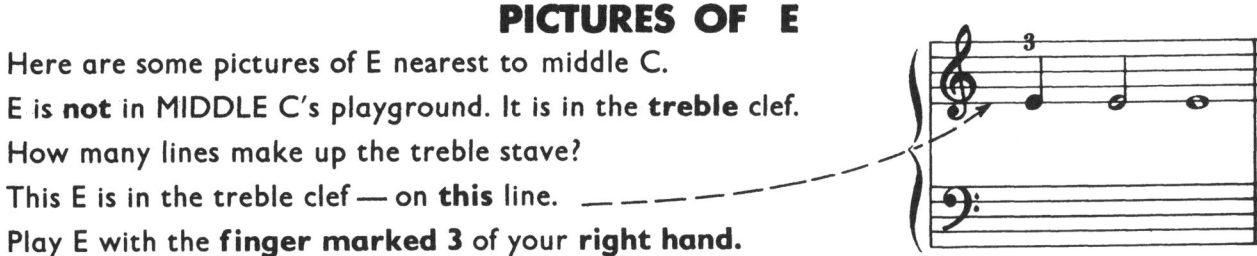

Here are some pictures of E nearest to middle C.
E is **not** in MIDDLE C's playground. It is in the **treble** clef.
How many lines make up the treble stave?
This E is in the treble clef — on **this** line.
Play E with the **finger marked 3** of your **right hand**.

Sing E as you play it. Here are some pieces for you to play.

SING TO ME

Remember the numbers that follow the clef signs!

The **top** figure is the one you must remember!

Count 1, 2 in every bar!

Teacher's Part

W. M. Co., 8448

Here is another piece for you to play.

THE SHOE COBBLER

THE RAIN

A ON KEYBOARD

Find the white note to the **left** of B.

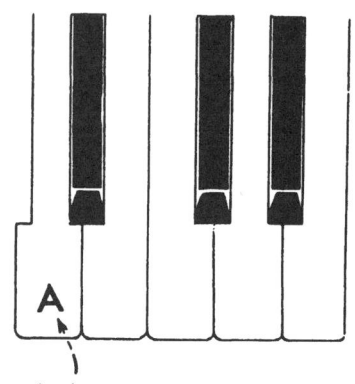

This is A

Play A with the **finger marked 3** of your **left** hand.

Sing A as you play it.

W. M. Co., 8448

Here are some pictures of A nearest to Middle C.

A is **not** in MIDDLE C's playground. It is in the **bass** clef.

How many lines make up the **bass** stave?

This A is in the bass clef — on **this** line.

Play A with the **finger marked 3** of your **left hand**.

Sing A as you play it.

KITTY CAT

Kit - ty cat is sleep - ing. Sleep-ing in the sun.

Teacher's Part

IN THE SNOW

Down I go, In the snow.

Teacher's Part

TWO SINGING

Right hand is Mother's voice.
Left hand is Father's voice.

Moth - er sings and Fath - er sings, and now they sing to - geth - er.

Teacher's Part

W. M. Co., 8448

CROSSING THE CREEK

Here is a little creek. Each circle is a rock. Write the name of each note in the circle. See if you can cross the creek without getting your feet wet!

Any mistake means you step in the water!

BIRTHDAY CAKES

Here are birthday cakes that need candles.

Put as many candles on each cake as there are **counts** in the **notes** on the cake.

A note like this ♩ gets **one** count.   The first one is done to show you how to do the others.

W. M. Co., 8448

SOLDIERS

Each soldier beats **four bars** on his drum.

The soldier is beating either $\frac{2}{4}$ or $\frac{4}{4}$ time.

Write the **time signature** before each line.

Write the **counts** under each note. Like this

You have had pieces
with **two** counts in a bar.

You have had pieces with
four counts in a bar.

Notice the **top** number in this time signature.

This means that you must count 1, 2, 3, in **each** bar.

You know that a note like this 𝅗𝅥 sings long enough for you to count 1, 2

When a note like this has a dot after it 𝅗𝅥. it sings long enough for you to count 1, 2, 3

Here are some pieces for you to play.

NORTH WIND

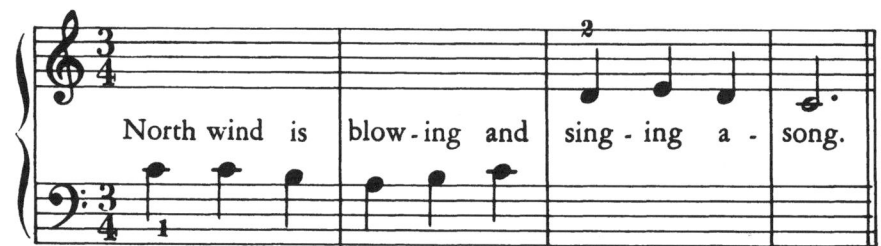

North wind is blow-ing and sing-ing a - song.

Did you remember to count 1, 2, 3, for the last note?

Teacher's Part

W. M. Co., 8448

A TIE

When two notes of the same pitch (sound) are shown connected with a curved line like this ♩‿♩ or ♩‿♩ it is called a **tie**.

This means you must play the **first** note, and **HOLD** the second giving it a count to its full value as crotchet, minim, or semibreve.

DO NOT LIFT YOUR HAND AND PLAY THE SECOND (or tied) NOTE AGAIN.

Here are some **ties**.

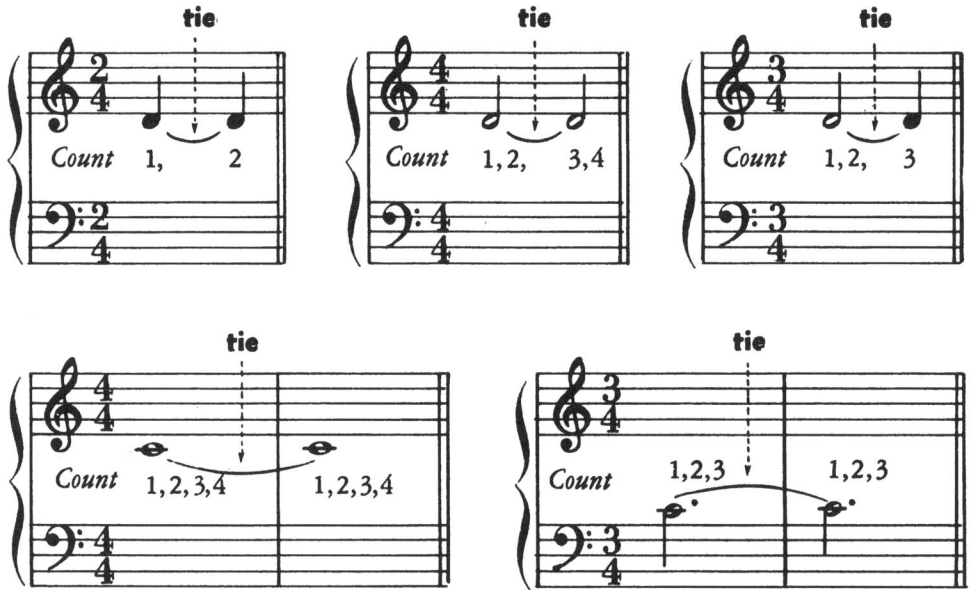

Here are some pieces with **ties**. Point them out.

BESSY COW

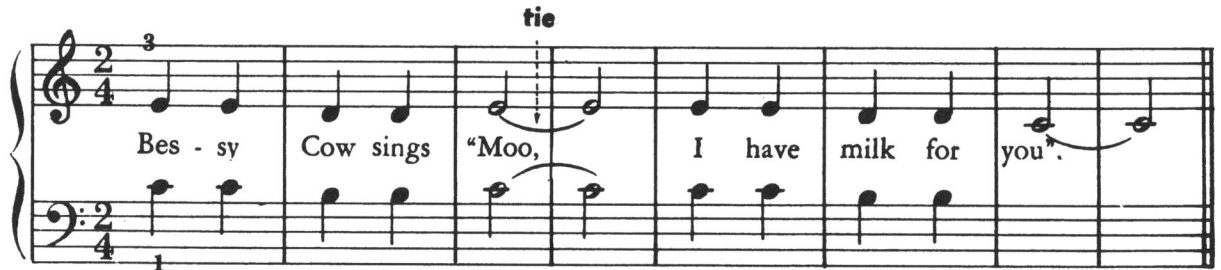

Point out the **ties** in the Teacher's part.

W. M. Co., 8448

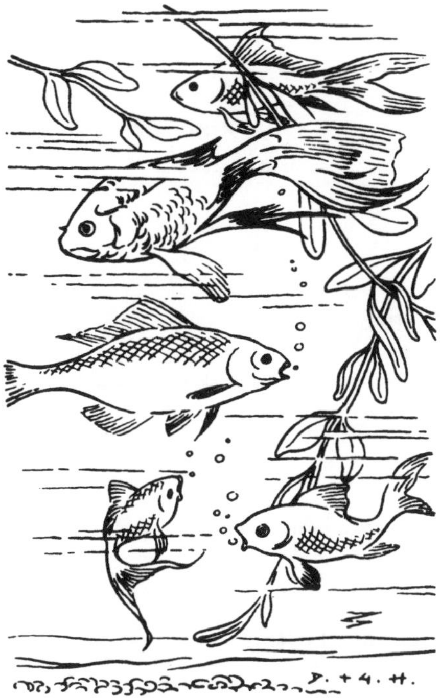

GOLDFISH

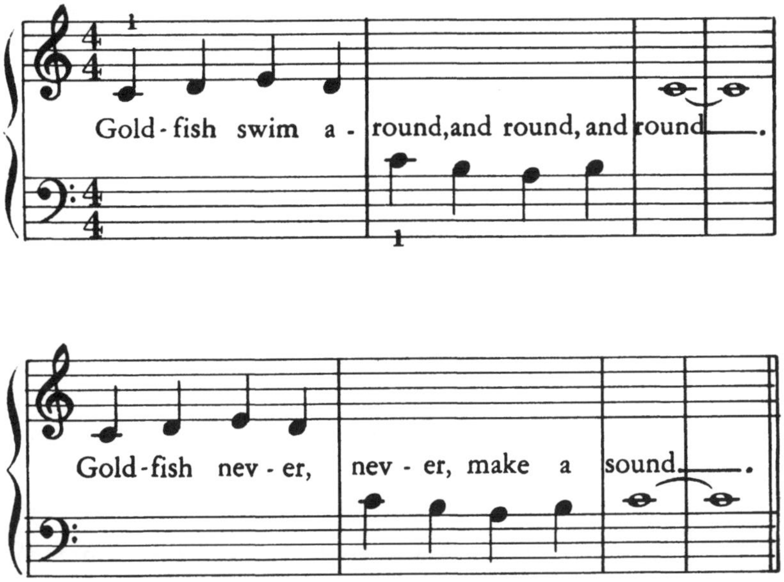

Teacher's Part

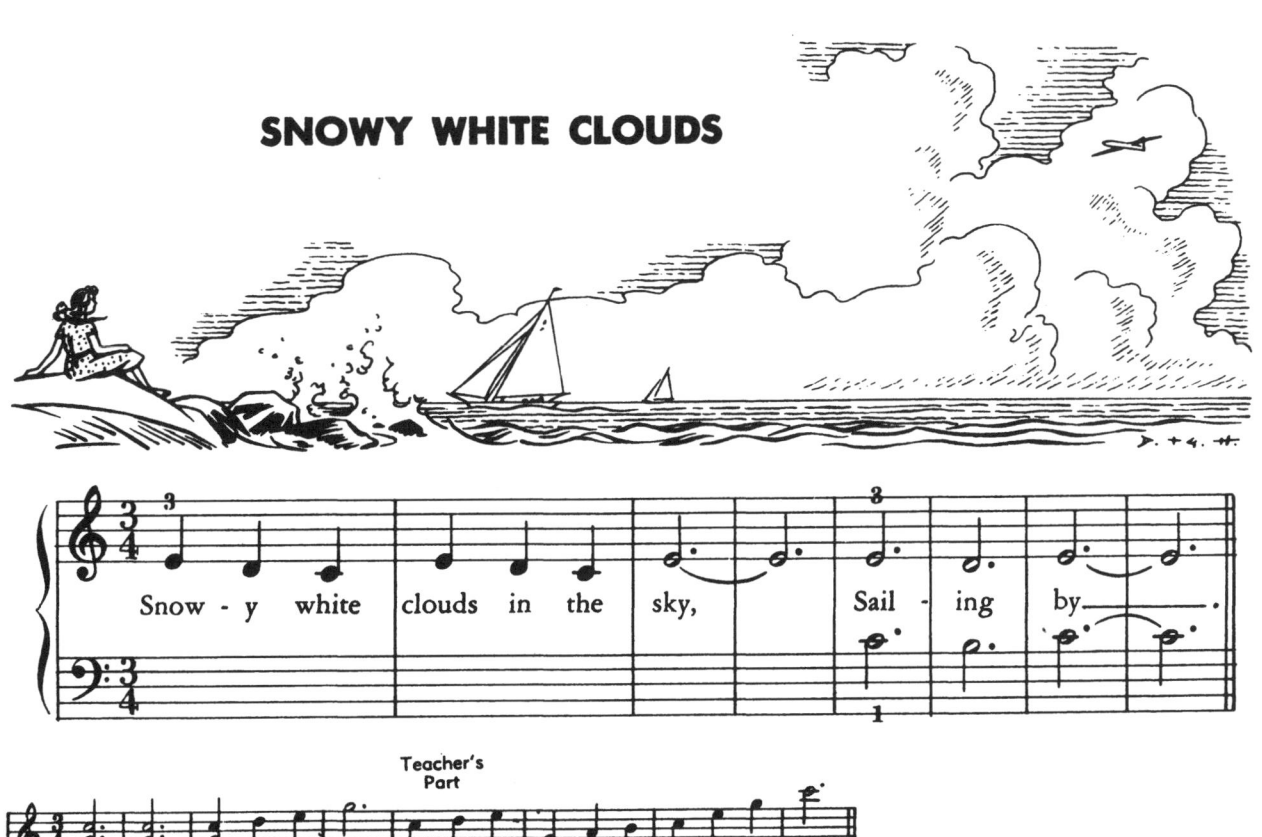

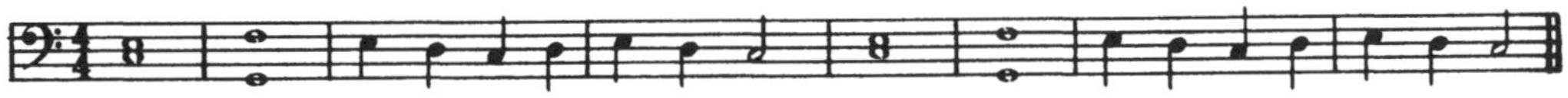

SNOWY WHITE CLOUDS

Teacher's Part

ONE-COUNT RESTS
CROTCHET-RESTS
A rest is a sign of silence.

This is a **crotchet** rest.

This kind of rest gets **one** count.

When you see a rest sign you must lift your hand from the keyboard and **count** to the time-value of the rest.

Here is a piece that has some **one** count (crotchet) rests.

JUMP ROPE

Count   1,   2,   3,   4

Your hands do not always rest at the **same** time.

Sometimes they take **turns** resting. Play the piece below.

HOP SCOTCH

W. M. Co., 8448

TWO-COUNT RESTS
MINIM-RESTS

29

This kind of rest gets **two** counts.

It sits on the **middle** line of each stave.

This is a **minim** rest.

Here is a piece that has some two count (minim) rests.

ROCKING CHAIR

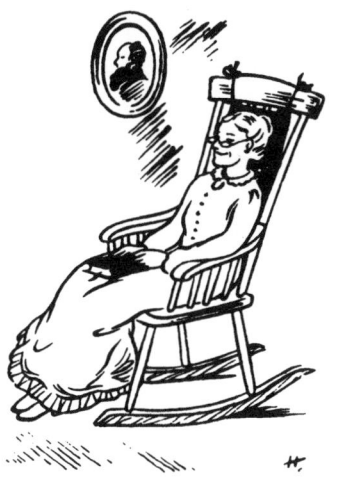

REVIEW

This piece has some **one** count rests and **also** some **two** count rests.

BUMPY STREETS

W. M. Co., 8448

FOUR-COUNT RESTS
SEMIBREVE RESTS

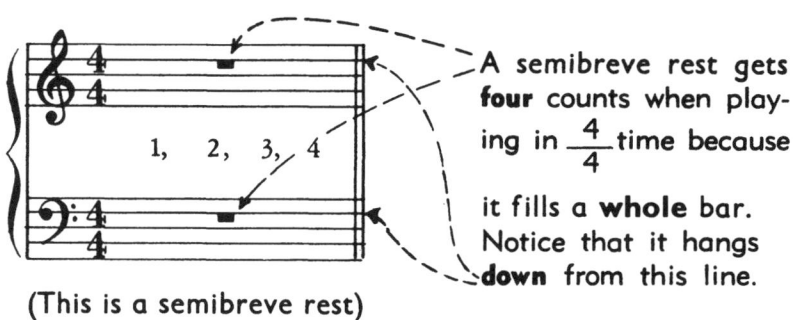

(This is a semibreve rest)

A semibreve rest gets **four** counts when playing in $\frac{4}{4}$ time because it fills a **whole** bar. Notice that it hangs **down** from this line.

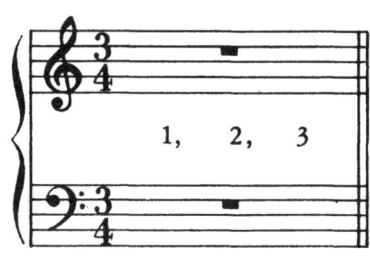

(Semibreve rest)

When playing in $\frac{3}{4}$ time this same kind of rest gets **three** counts because it fills the whole bar.

SHEEP

Sheep are stand-ing on a hill, and they stand ver-y still.

WHEELS

Wheels go a-round and a-round___ Wheels go all ov-er the ground.___

Did you remember to count the tied notes?

W. M. Co., 8448

Here is a piece that has **all** of the different kinds of rests you have learned.
Try a four-count **sigh** at the empty bars while waiting!

LATE DELIVERY

F ON KEYBOARD

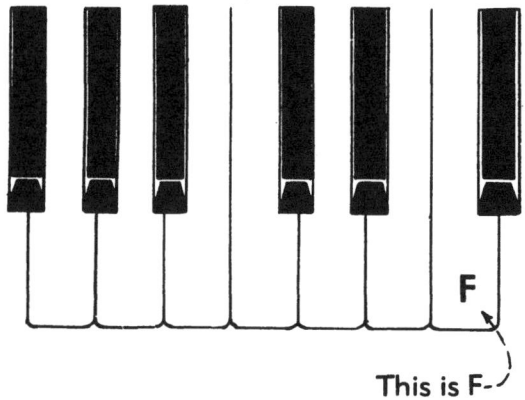

Find the white note to the **right** of E

This is F

Here are some pictures of F nearest to Middle C.

F is **not** in MIDDLE C's playground.

It is in the **treble** clef.

Remember that the places **between** the lines. are called **spaces**.

How many spaces are shown on the treble stave?

This F is in the treble clef and in **this** space.

Play F with the **finger marked 4** of your **right** hand.

Sing F as you play it.

Here is a piece for you to play introducing the new note.

THE NIGHT

When I go out-side and look in-to the night.

I can see the stars, All beau-ti-ful and bright.

CORN ON THE COB

33

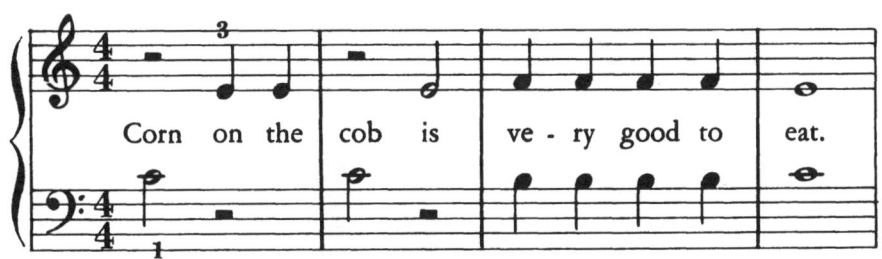
Corn on the cob is ve-ry good to eat.

Nib-ble, nib-ble, nib-ble, Eve-ry bite is sweet.

COUNTING SHEEP

Nod-ding my head as I count white sheep, Bab-y's the one who is now a-sleep.

W. M. Co., 8448

G BELOW MIDDLE C – ON KEYBOARD

Find the white note to the **left** of A (Below MIDDLE C)

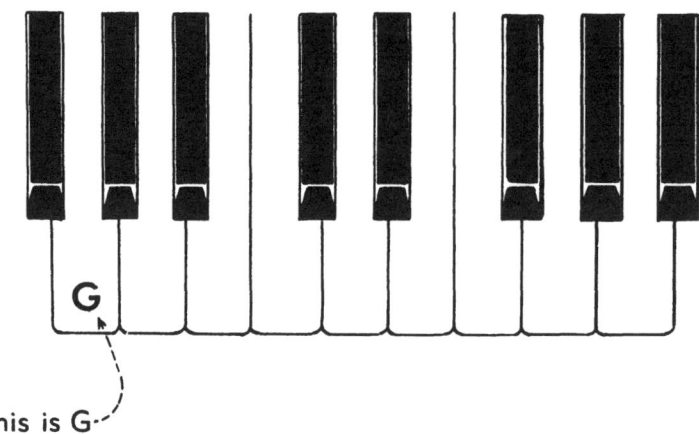

This is G

Play G with the **finger marked 4** of your **left** hand.

Sing G as you play it.

Here are some pictures of G for the **left** hand.

This G is in the **bass** clef.

It is in **this** space of the bass stave.

LITTLE RIVER

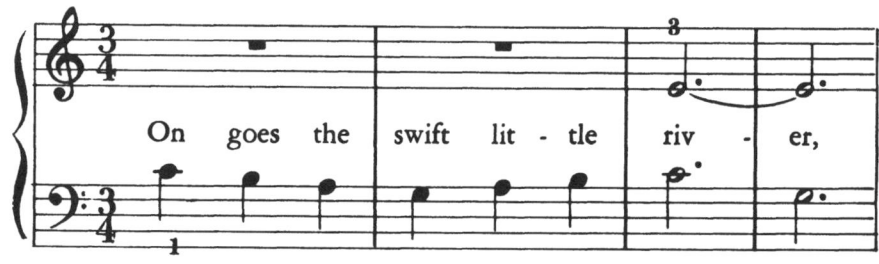

On goes the swift lit-tle riv-er,

Remember! Hold and count the tied notes to their full musical value.

Flow-ing right out to the sea.

W. M. Co., 8448

EVENING

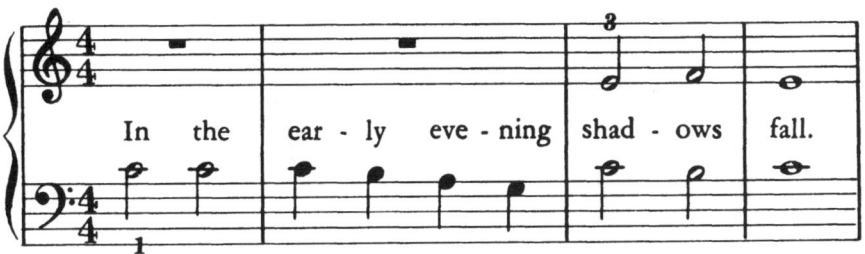

In the ear-ly eve-ning shad-ows fall.

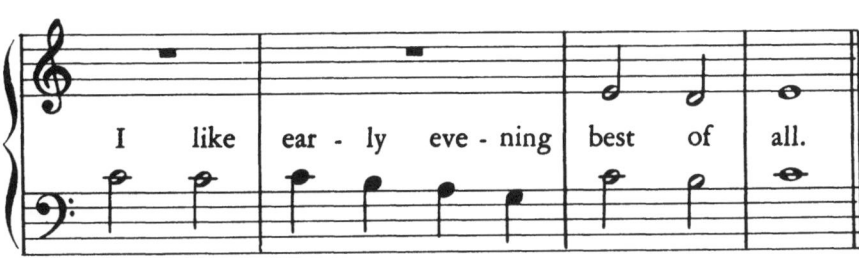

I like ear-ly eve-ning best of all.

LONDON BRIDGE

Lon-don bridge is fall-ing down, Fall-ing down, Fall-ing down,

Lon-don bridge is fall-ing down, My Fair Lad-y-o.

G ABOVE MIDDLE C – ON KEYBOARD

Find the white note to the **right** of F.
(Above MIDDLE C)

This is G

Here are some pictures of G for the **right** hand.

It is on **this** line of the **treble** stave.

Play this G with the **finger marked five** of your **right** hand.

Sing G as you play it.

HILLS

Hills go up and hills go down all in and out the ci-ty. Hills go up and hills go down and they are ver-y pret-ty.

W. M. Co., 8448

A SKYLINE THOUGHT
ON T.V. AERIALS

High on the house-tops, reach-ing to the sky,
Key to fresh mar-vels, screened from far and nigh.

MARY HAD A LITTLE LAMB

Mar-y had a lit-tle lamb, lit-tle lamb, lit-tle lamb.

Mar-y had a lit-tle lamb, Its fleece was white as snow.

W. M. Co., 8448

TWO CHILDREN HUMMING

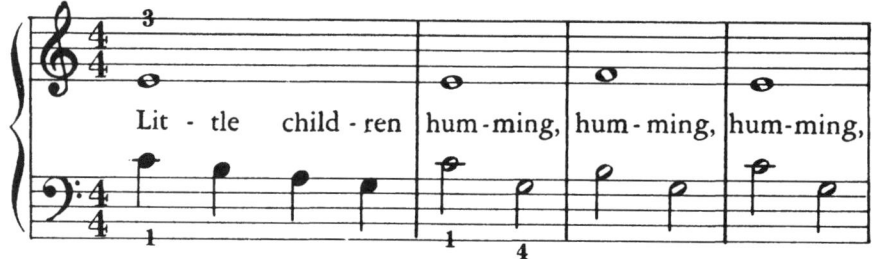
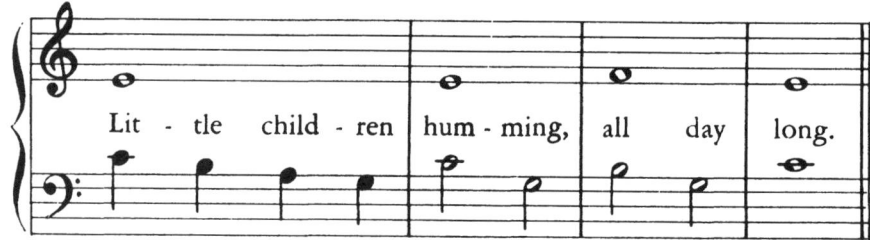

SUNSET

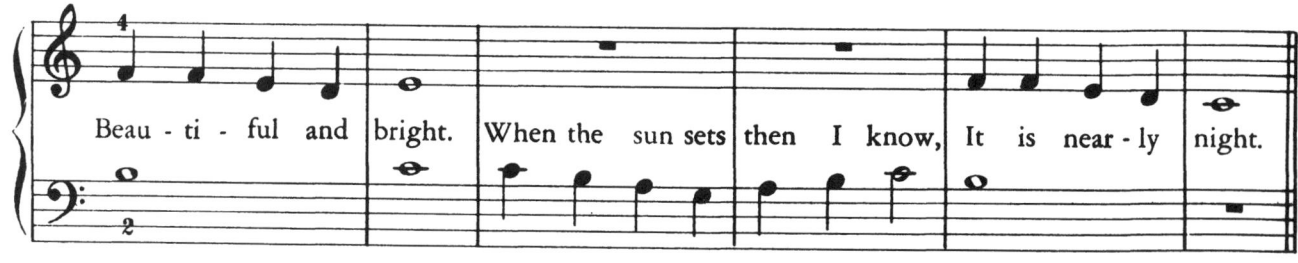

FISHING

Draw a fishing line from each pole to the fish it should catch.

If the pole is marked C, the line must go to the note C.

If you get it right it means you caught the fish!

See how many fish (notes) you can catch.

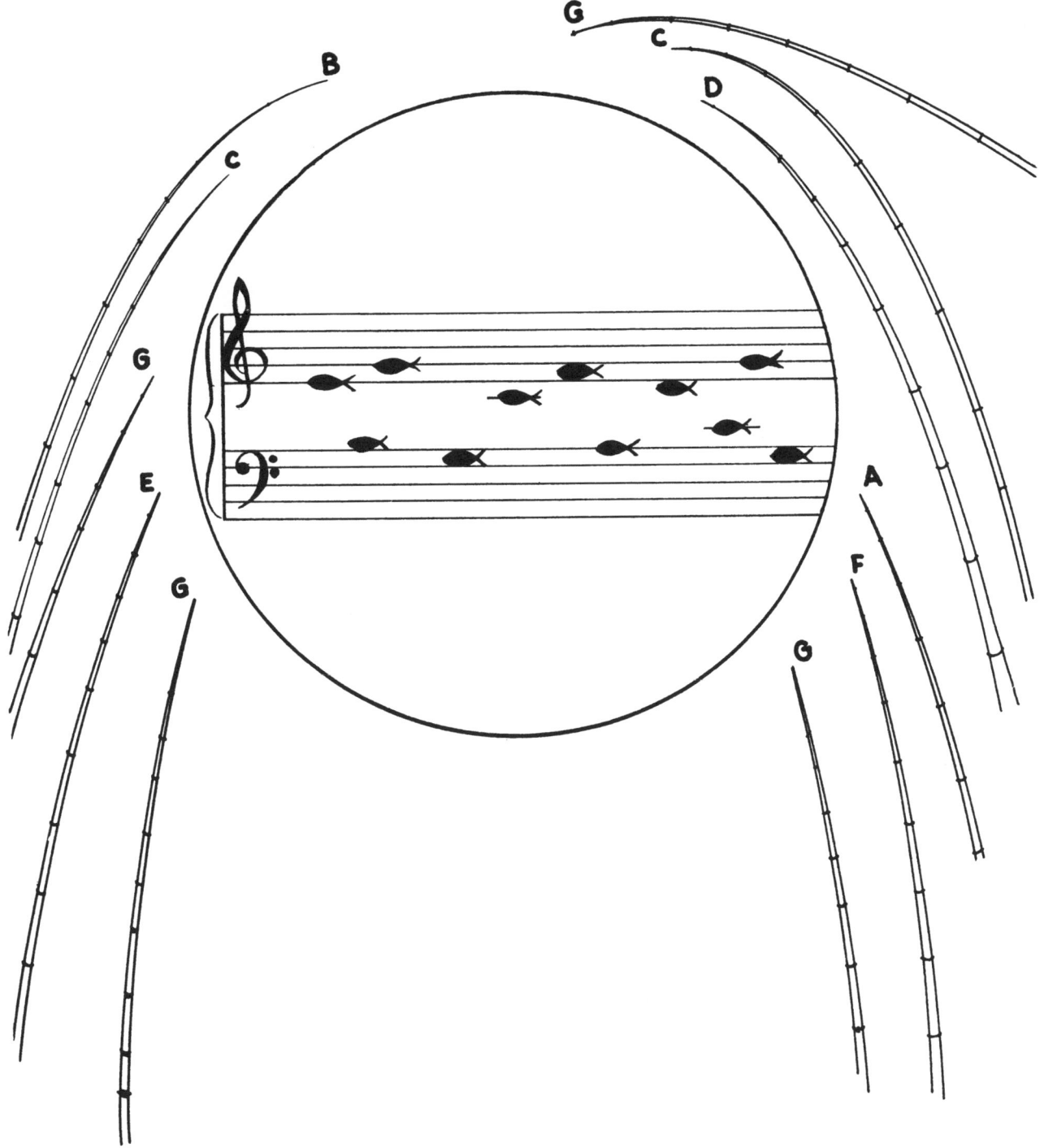

PENNIES IN A PURSE

Each purse has pennies inside it.

How many pennies are there in each purse?

There are as many pennies as there are counts to the notes.

Write the number of counts in each purse.

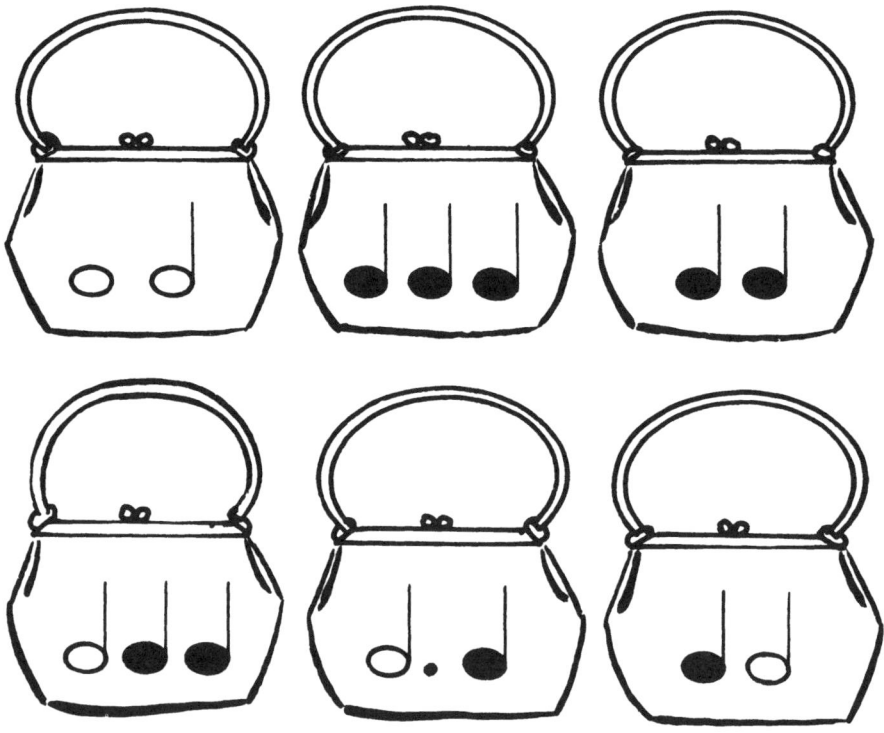

This time count the **notes and rests.**

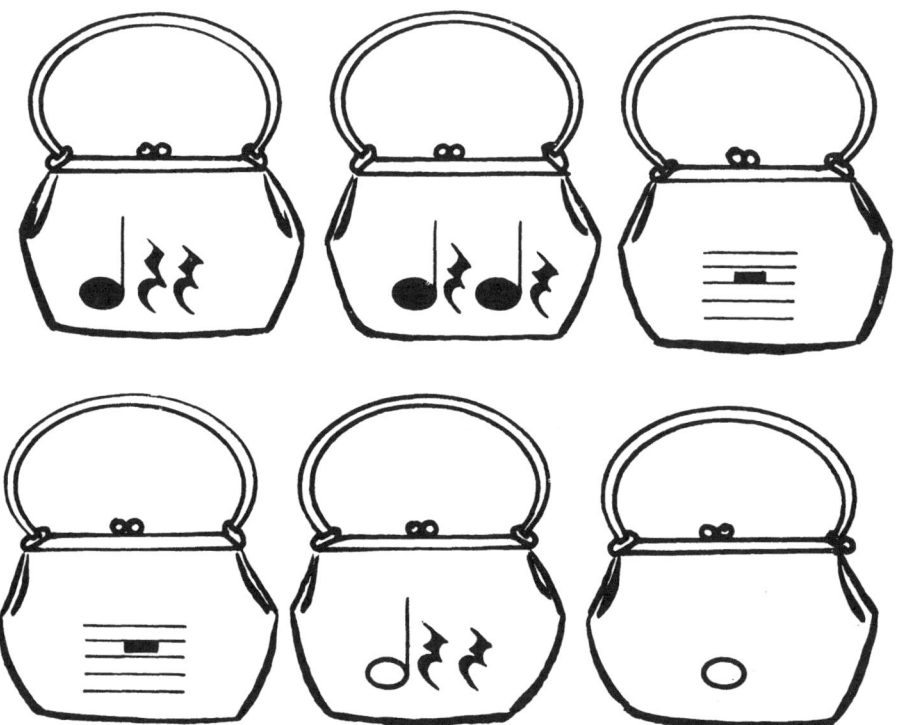

DUCKS

Each duck quacks four bars.

They quack in either $\frac{2}{4}$ $\frac{3}{4}$ or $\frac{4}{4}$ time.

Write the correct time signature before each line.

Then write the **counts** under the **notes** or **rests**.

Like this:—

LITTLE WHITE CHICKENS

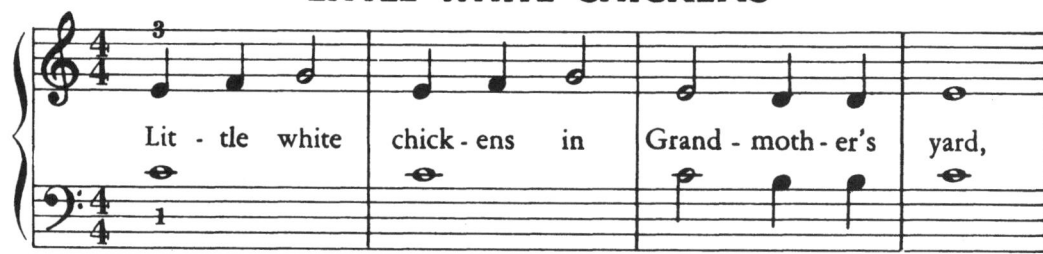

SOUTH WIND

GOING NORTH

L. W. D.

From Land's End to John O' Groats, the road-way twists and turns.

Leav-ing low-lands, reach-ing high-lands where dwelt Rob-ert Burns.

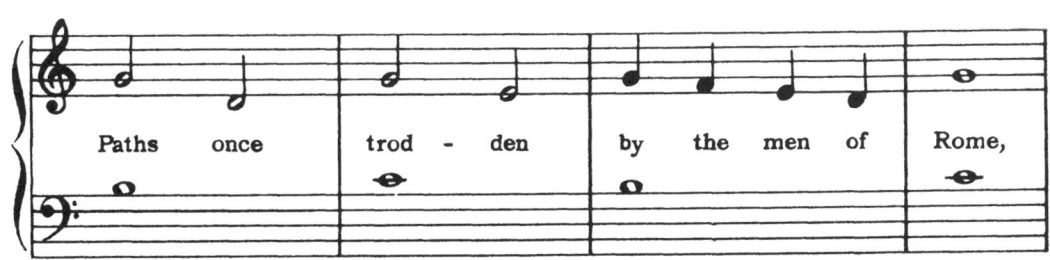
Paths once trod-den by the men of Rome,

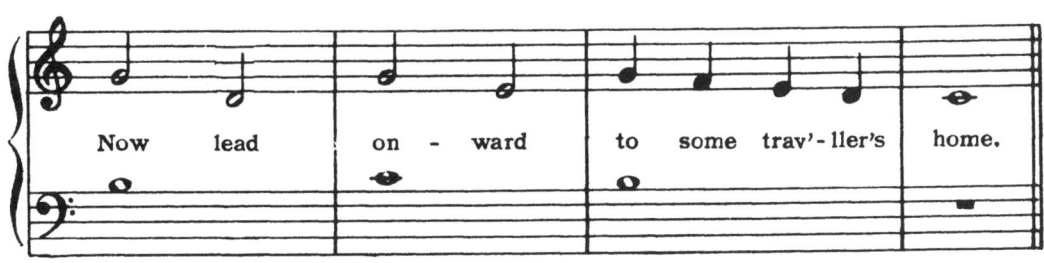
Now lead on-ward to some trav'-ller's home.

MINISTEPS TO MUSIC - Phase I. Review

How are the fingers numbered for playing the piano?

Describe the purpose of :—
- treble clef
- bass clef
- grand staff
- bar-line
- bar
- double-bar
- brace
- time signature

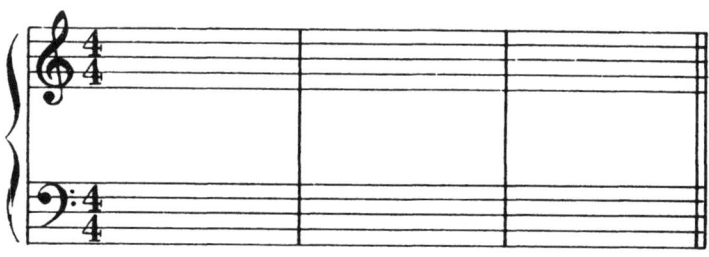

Which notes require the following counts? :—
- 1 count
- 2 counts
- 3 counts
- 4 counts

Which rests require the following counts :—
- 1 count
- 2 counts
- 4 counts

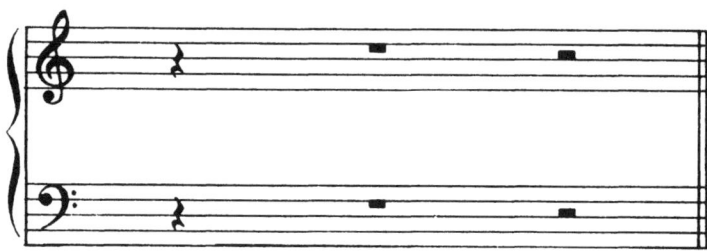

Which time signature defines the following counts? :—
- 2 counts to each bar
- 4 counts to each bar
- 3 counts to each bar

Explain the use of a tie

W. M. Co., 8448